Mario Mantese

You Are the World

Mario Mantese

# You Are the World

## Pearls of Love

Translated from the German by Mark Doyu Albin
Edited by Doris Hüffer-Schott
Typesetting and Cover design by Marion Musenbichler
Cover illustration © fotolia.com/alexilly
Photograph Mario Mantese © by Günther Ciupka

Original Title: Die Welt bist Du
© 1994 Mario Mantese, first published
by Drei Eichen Verlag, D-97762 Hammelburg
© 2015 Edition Spuren
Bahnhofsplatz 14, CH-8400 Winterthur

Bibliographical Information of the German National Library
This publication is listed in the German National Bibliography of the
German National Library; detailed bibliographical information
can be accessed under http://dnb.d-nb.de

ISBN: 978-3-7431-0454-9

© 2017 by Mario Mantese
www.mariomantese.com

First Edition in English
Printing and Production by BoD – Books on Demand, Norderstedt

# The Birth of Light

Don't you know that it is me who looks through your eyes, and me who smiles upon you as colorful, fragrant flowers along your path? Don't you know that it is me who warms you as the warmth in fire, and that I am the coolness in the wind that whispers and caresses?

I, the All-encompassing, All-penetrating, love you boundlessly. You are a precious limb of my formless light-body.

My thoughts of love allowed you to become flesh, and I have provided you with unlimited wisdom and power, and with creative will, so you can express this glory and perfection in infinite diversity.

Never for a moment did I stray from you, Beloved, for you are a part of me – yes, you are me myself. Why have you turned away from me and misused my powers? Why did you ever give life to those thoughts of death and crystallize them, when in truth you are immortal and unborn in me, eternally pure and immaculate? Why did you use my creative powers of imagination to produce a world separate from me, a frightening, dark, heartless world? Even when you have lost sight of me, never for a moment have I strayed from you. My love for you is unwavering and eternally steadfast.

With my power you have set a law in motion that is outside of me, where you have made yourself prisoner; a law of self-seeking, of destiny. Although I am also the power within this law, I am not this law, for it was set in motion by the heartlessness of your selfish pursuits – condensing and restricting material instead of releasing it.

I have supplied you with everything, with my complete and unconditional love. Why do you seek something else; why do you create separation? I am not yesterday nor tomorrow; I am always *now*. Why do you constantly move away from me, Beloved?

I see your dark thoughts; how you contemplate ideas of death and rebirth, and how you believe and attach yourself to these thoughts and ideas. Why have you moved away from this endless purity and clarity, and believe in things like life, death, and re-birth, when you are, in truth, immortal and boundless? Life, death, and re-birth are nothing but concepts in your divided, darkened consciousness.

You have fashioned cultures, religions and political systems outside of me, and your thoughts and beliefs adhere tightly to them. You are convinced that these invented, relative thought-structures are reality.

See how they fluctuate, see their impermanence, and know that they have no existence within me. All these things have existence only during the moments you think about them. Otherwise they are non-existent, nothing more that fleeting shadows.

I continuously see into your darkened heart, which can no longer distinguish between me and its own self-seeking, with all its stifling hardships. Why do you turn away from me: universal, all-embracing love?

Don't you see that my love never increases or decreases, that it is always complete in all things and through all things? Have you forgotten that I have embellished and glorified you with the ultimate gift of love? Truly, you are a cherished limb of my formless cosmic body.

Why do you cause so much commotion, and create so much confusion? Nevertheless, I live within you as eternal peace and everlasting stillness. Yet, you have used my power to create a peculiar shadow-world, where you believe you must absolutely prove yourself.

You use my word, my boundless power of love; you bend it to lead wars in my name, to murder, to torture, and to betray. Have you forgotten that there is absolutely no shadow within me, and no such thoughts have ever arisen? I am pure light and perfect peace; perfect justice. I am the law itself.

I am no judge, and you will never be judged by me, for my all-encompassing love has pardoned you of all your mistakes before you made them. The suffering that befalls you is nothing but the constant corrective of my love, which purifies and restores you when you have distanced yourself far away from me.

Have you forgotten that your true being is boundless purity and health; that within you there was, in truth, never the slightest seed of sickness, and never will be? For you are me, and I am you, eternally perfect.

Suffering and worry are like clouds floating by in the sky. No matter how thick the cloud cover is, the sun continues to shine, and the wind chases the clouds away again. Why do you only watch your body, your thoughts, and your feelings? They are like clouds passing by.

Why don't you look at me, who resides within you, who infuses you and gives you life, who burns hotter than a thousand suns?

Because you cannot perceive me with your instruments of sense, you believe I exist externally, outside the transient body. But this thought is nothing but a dream of yours. Awaken now in me, Beloved, and live your life completely unfettered in light, love, and total freedom.

Still, you believe that I am also your dream. Awaken, and you will recognize that your dream never existed, for I am real. You look for me in your yesterday and do not find me, because a yesterday never existed within me.

You hope for a tomorrow, and with this hope you constantly distance yourself from me. But you can never become me or reach me, because I am eternally *now*. Never was there something before and after me, for I am endless and beginningless.

I listen to your prayers, your invocations and pleadings, but only in the everlasting silence of your heart can you find me, there where your prayers are fulfilled before you ever thought of them or uttered them. Indeed, your prayers are mostly aimed at harmonizing your darkness, to brighten your world a little more.

As long as you are not completely ready to look at me face to face, so I can completely dispel and expel your darkness, you will continue to live in your world of shadows. Here, you have taken the powers of love from me, and used and misused them for your own self-avowing life.

I am not cross with you, for my all-embracing love is universal compassion and mercy. When can I hold you in my arms entirely once again, Beloved? I do not force you, nor do I pressure you, for I am universal understanding itself. My love is absolute and unconditional. When you turn to me with all your love, all your worries, illnesses, and anxieties melt away like ice under the sun.

Also when you have murdered; in thoughts, in feelings, or in action, it is always the power of love which you have misused. With this deed, as with countless others, you have set an inferior law in motion, a law outside of me. This is the law of karma, of action, reaction, and counter reaction.

In this way you have produced the forces of destiny and bound yourself to them, for they are you yourself. Oh Beloved, you have set so much in motion through this distortion of my powers of love that you can no longer see me, and no longer even believe that I am!

Don't you know that without me not one single thought can arise within you, that you cannot raise nor close your eyelids, that no word comes over your lips, and that no sound can be heard?

I am the eternal thinker itself, and also the listener who hears through your ears. What do *you* believe perceives beauty and basks in delight? In your darkness, your subjective evaluating, criticizing manner, you have carved the beauty and tenderness of my revelations into pieces, cheapened them, dulled them, and thus mutilated my cosmic countenance.

Don't you see the immeasurable beauty in the minuscule as well as in the enormous? Don't you see that it is I who live in the small as well as in the big, that I permeate all with my love? Don't you see how I breathe through and listen to all beings at the same time, how I move all things and everything? There is only one breath, only one creation, and I am that myself. I am the creator and the maintainer, as well as the power which dispels my flesh-forming thoughts.

The transitory only seems to be transitory, for truly I am unborn and formless. Awaken, Beloved, and look straight into my eyes. What are you afraid of? See that the dreamer and what was dreamed are only ideas in your world of concepts, in your imagination. For truly I am beyond waking-states or dream-states: I am the eternally silent observer in you.

I am the light in your eyes, and yet, you cannot see me. But that, Beloved, is nothing for you to worry about. For the world which you observe with the external sensory organs is itself a reflection of me. Still, do not forget: the image that appears in the mirror is only a reflection, and not my eternally inconceivable reality. Recognize yourself!

When you have cleansed your heart of the dust-like impermanence of this world, it will be luminously pure and clear like a crystal mirror. In this mirror you will look at me face to face, and know that I was here eternally, and that there is no difference between us.

The world that originates in me appears to you like a dream, because you have separated yourself from me, and can no longer recognize my wholeness and my indivisibility. Because you ceaselessly separate yourself from me in your self-asserting and egoistic way, your life has become a bad dream, and you have continued to distance yourself from me even further, without ever noticing.

Do not forget: my unending, all-encompassing power of love is also the law, and everything that has fallen into disorder will be corrected, reformed, and purified. For I am the Great

Order itself, which you will be relentlessly called back to. When your heart is dulled and hardened, my law of love seems severe and cruel. When your heart is soft and pure, you know that this law guides you with graceful, steady wings back into my boundless heart. I have not invented this law. I am this eternal law itself, abundant with compassion and mercy.

When you have separated yourself from me due to your self-seeking, and are bound to your dark corridors of thought, you create ambiguity, disharmony, and illness. And this is expressed on all levels of your physical form.

This is no punishment of mine. Rather, it is your own, one you encourage yourself, for every cause has its effect. Know that your stomach pains, your headaches and toothaches, and also all your heavy burdens and sufferings do not leave any stain or scar on me. They do not affect me, although I am you, Beloved. I live in each cell and each atom within you, and yet I am completely inviolable against disharmony and sickness.

My compassion and my comprehensive love fill you constantly, and instill you with my immeasurable power. Why do you not turn completely and face me, so I can remove all your shadows?

Why are you so angry with me, and make me responsible for all that is bad in the world? Have I turned away from the world, or the world from me, the universal law? You misuse my endless power of love in order to plant fear and terror, and you make me responsible for this. Thus, you have lost your faith in me. You have gone so far as to convince yourself that I do not exist, and that I never existed.

Why don't you awaken from your dream? I am eternally at your side, always full of love. I could never leave you, for you are a valuable limb of my formless cosmic body.

In your shadow-world, where there are also bright, cheerful moments, you are loving and kind at times, and think that you are therefore closer to me. Know, Beloved, that when you encounter my diversity, whether my expression be black, white, yellow or red, or any other colorful hue of the body's appearance, if there are uncertainties and mixed feelings in your heart, then your loving and your kindness are nothing but gray zones in your world of shadows.

Know that I live completely untainted and pure in you, and I know neither separation nor preference, because all creatures are valuable limbs of my cosmic light-body.

Understand my all-embracing love, and be it as well. Then you fulfill the cosmic law of love. Yes, then you are the law of love itself. See the immeasurable tenderness and boundless supremacy of this law. I fill you ceaselessly with my flow of grace, and cleanse you of all earthly attachments with my vital waters.

Become porous for my love. Be without shadows, just as I am. In this way my unlimited flow of love will flow through you and radiate outwards. The entire span of the shadow-world will then be illuminated and transformed. For you know: where there is light, darkness ceases to exist.

In this way, Beloved, you are in perfect accordance with me. Countless beings will be attracted by the power of love, as if pulled by a colossal, illuminating magnet. In this way my beloved ones continuously return to my beginningless heart. Take delight in my infinite love!

Do not forget, Beloved: you do the thinking, but I am the great navigator. Be very attentive to what things abide in your creative thoughts, for what you think is what you are. Be conscious that you borrow the power to think from me. Do not misuse it; do not twist it, for this allows the dark and obstinate things of the shadow-world to arise.

How liberating and healing for the world! Attune the flow of your thoughts completely to me, the unbounded cosmic law of love! Love all things and everything unconditionally, and all things and everything will love you unconditionally.

I am the Father of all lights; I am the Mother of all creatures. I am the Logos, the essence of wisdom, and wisdom itself. Do not forget: because I am *that*, you are *that* as well. However, your selfishness has constructed a light-barrier between you and myself, and you live only in a shadow of me, who is limitless, begininningless love.

The world, time, and space are not existent within me, although I am in them. The moon revolves around the planet Earth, and the Earth itself rotates and revolves around the sun. All the planets with their moons circle around the sun in a huge electromagnetic field. The sun and the entire system of celestial bodies which it vitalizes, nourishes and maintains, also revolve in a tremendous cycle, drawn by a still greater electromagnetic field and a central sun in the Milky Way. And the Milky Way itself is embedded in a still larger, more powerful gathering of galactic systems.

Know me as a comprehensive energy field, where material is condensed and dispersed in an interplay of numerous forces. I am that which lives in your mind and grants you the power to contemplate the universe.

The universe did not arise through coincidence. You did not appear through coincidence. Everything contains and is my complex order.

There is interaction between all atoms in the universe. My nature is one inseparable whole, wherein everything is in connection with everything else. See yourself in me, Beloved!

You cannot observe the physical world without influencing it, for you cannot stand apart, isolated from reality. You participate fully.

It is all my constantly changing face. I am the mover and also the moved, and I am the immortal intelligence in the movement. You, Beloved, are a part of my imageless, formless body.

You call me *Mother*, and truly, I am the all-loving, all-embracing, all-engendering power of love; life itself, which gives birth to itself eternally.

You call me *Father*, and I am that. I am will and wisdom and the power of perfect integration and unification; that which creates all of life. But I am not dualistic, not twofold. Rather, I am all-pervasive Spirit; complete union itself.

My love is undivided in the smallest as well as in the largest. The affectionate gaze of a mother upon her newborn child is the same amongst all living beings. I am that which looks through these eyes, loving and protecting all creatures.

I gaze out with these loving eyes in the same way through all mothers in the animal world who give birth, and I gaze out in the same manner with these loving eyes through all human mothers who give birth. It is with one and the same loving gaze that I look out – without even the slightest variance – through every living being.

My space is filled with creatures and living beings of immeasurable variety. I have put the animals under your care for you to protect and love. They are your friends, and they share the same realm with you.

Why then, do you kill them and ravage their flesh, rip their skin from their bodies, and even eat their bowels, their sexual organs, and their hearts?

You brutally tear young animals away from their mothers and take them to slaughterhouses, causing the same suffering a human being suffers when a child is wrested from its mother and killed. Have you forgotten that I am the one who lives in all creatures? Oh, you thoughtless, world-weary One! Awaken, and open your clouded eyes! Love and respect all creatures, for all creatures are me.

You pray to me, and at the same time you kill me. You kill my animals, which I have placed in the same domain as you with my universal love. Because you are stronger, and appear to be clever enough, you treat them brutally, with total disrespect.

You kill millions of my loved ones daily. As the butcher takes hold of them, their loud, lamenting, terror-filled cries of fear permeate the world day and night. If those animals could weep, the entire earth would be flooded, and your fields and orchards would be submerged in bloody tears. Are you aware that each year more than 1.5 billion large animals and 22.5 billion birds are butchered, and that each year billions of fish are snatched from their element, water, and wretchedly suffocated?

Awaken, Beloved, cleanse and clarify your dark and dulled heart, and see how far you have distanced yourself from me. Why don't you raise yourself up? Why don't you awaken?

Humans kill humans: humans abuse and mutilate humans in unimaginable ways. If the fear, the pain, and the doubt of these people would be visible to all, amassed together in one dark cloud, you would live in complete darkness. No sunlight would ever reach the planet Earth.

Why do you kill, misuse, and mutilate in your actions, in your mind, in your thoughts and feelings, Beloved? Awaken and see how far you have distanced yourself from me. What have you done with my universal power of love, oh Irresponsible One?

Do not believe that there is a difference between humans and animals, for I am all creatures. Here, only your darkened, self-righteous heart causes you to see a difference where there is none. Awaken, Beloved, break through the thick black crust covering your heart - beyond it, I am there.

Your self-seeking has blinded you while your eyes are open, and robbed you of your pure faculty of discernment. How hardhearted you have become with me, the Father of all lights, the Mother of all creatures. I never scold you nor punish you, but I see into your heart, and witness how you ceaselessly punish yourself and suffer, and how you, in the inner dimness of your life's progression, live in conflict with yourself.

Your heart is restless, full of fear and anxiety, and you make great efforts to hide it. Dear Beloved, why don't you transform yourself with me into light? You can then be assured that all your self-generated fears and doubts will dissolve into nothing.

I am the unborn, and also that which is born, born from itself. I am the resurrecting power of nature in spring, and the resurrecting power in you, oh Beloved. Although I am formless, I reveal myself through myself as form: I, the inseparable eternal Self. I am inseparable life, within the large as well as the small.

Beloved, haven't you seen by now that I am you and you are me, and that there is absolutely no difference between us? You are me.

You search for me incessantly, as if I was something foreign to you. Your searching, your thinking, and your concepts lead you continually further away from me, who is the closest of all that is close to you. You yourself create this estrangement, and search for solutions to the problem of finding me. But you never find me, the closest one of all.

You seek without knowing what you are actually looking for. You have produced countless religions and philosophies, and invented all kinds of mystical systems; yet you do not find me, the nearest of all, for all your searching has led you away from me.

You have never dared to search for the seeker. You are afraid of the Great Silence. You fear yourself; you who are the Great Silence. Know this: the silence that is perceived as silence is not the last eternal silence.

As long as you seek me, you will not find me, and when you stop searching for me, you will also not find me. Recognize me as the nearest of all, the eternal Now!

I am beyond becoming, wanting, and having, beyond everything you can imagine or not imagine, beyond the impermanent and the permanent. I know neither life nor death, for I am the Unborn; I am eternal being, the most imminent.

See me, Beloved, abide in me, in the eternal radiance of my boundless love! The stench of decay and decay itself are completely dissolved in me, the nearest of all. I have become flesh for you, so that I can reveal my infinite powers of love and transformation in immeasurable, splendid magnificence.

See yourself in me, Beloved, so that my power of revelation permeates your being! In this way the flesh is completely spiritualized and sanctified in me and through me, the most imminent.

From power to power, from splendor to splendor, raise yourself upon the wings of my immeasurable love. Beloved, you belong to me and not to time, oh Immortal Soul. You do not belong to the flesh, which is temporary. You, oh Soul, cannot be killed and cannot die. Yet, you have turned away from me, and covered yourself in the burial shroud of ignorance.

Recognize yourself, oh Mortal One! Know, Blessed One, that I am the king of kings, the king of the sun-like beings living in the eternal light-realm, equal in power to all the volcanoes on earth. Truly, they are the Anointed Ones, who bring my everlasting glory to expression in its full magnitude. Awaken, Beloved, recognize yourself!

I am the one thought from which all thoughts are revealed. I am the one feeling out of which all feelings arise. Do not lose yourself in apparent variety, for I alone am the great *unity*, outside of which nothing exists.

Do you believe, Beloved, that you could form even one tiny thought without me? I am the creator as well as creation; there is no barrier between us, no difference. There is not the one and the other. Rather, there is only me: indivisible Spirit.

You have used the free and unlimited will that underlies the essence of my love improperly. Thus, you have created separation from me, and this darkness distresses you. I know all beings, for all beings are me. You know neither me nor your neighbor, for you live trapped in your own isolation, which you yourself have created.

I hold out my hands of love constantly to you, and you do not see them, oh darkened Soul. Your stubbornness doesn't cause me pain; it is your own pain, which you consciously or unconsciously have inflicted on yourself through countless actions and reactions.

Know that I am beyond all actions, and yet, I am the cause of everything. Awaken, Beloved! Recognize your true home – boundless space.

I am the invisible, highly refined law, the willful goal of all life. Awaken, be in complete accordance with me, oh Soul, in cosmic harmony with my indivisible ever-presence! I am the eternal ocean of life, and you are my wave, who gently moves over me. This is how the visible world arises out of me, and how it disperses again within me.

Do not fall into delusion, Beloved! See and experience yourself as a wave which comes and goes. I am the great Whole. The wave is a smile from me, a smile so you can recognize me once again in my immeasurable love. Awaken and look at me face to face. Then all waves will be calmed in my great, motionless body of silence and light.

Through me you see, but you do not see me; through me you listen, but you do not hear me. Indeed, you are blind while seeing and deaf while listening, trapped in your own misunderstandings.

I am the light of life, the light within life itself. I am the Spirit of all life, the origin of the world and all concepts. I am not only the origin of the world, but also its framework, that which holds it together. I am its fiber, its actual Self.

I am the Lord of all worlds, the Creator. And I am the inexhaustible, tremendous, everlasting joy which is the impetus of my creation. I am the Lord of all worlds, father and mother of all gods, angels, human beings and every single creature. They are the diverse adornment of my unified body.

My flow of grace saturates all souls with my enlivening light. With my pure waters of love, I revive everything which lives in me. I am perfect equilibrium, eternal cosmic harmony. Why, Beloved, do you live in imbalance and disharmony with me? Realize the unnatural condition you are moving within.

You try to become one with me, and your becoming leads you further and further away from me. You can never become me, for I am always the Eternal, the Unbecoming, the timeless Now. See the snares of your seeking, Beloved, and awaken!

You should neither search for me, nor not search. Rather, you should recognize yourself in your true, timeless state. See then whether there is a difference between you and me.

All your linear searching produces time perpetually, and time means delusion and confinement. Confinement means life and death and the heavy chains of reincarnating the body; reincarnating your dullness, your own ignorance.

Know, Beloved, this all has nothing to do with me. The Infinite never involves itself with the finite, wisdom never touches ignorance, and darkness never mingles with light. I am eternal, ineffable, unthinkable *life* itself, beyond all ideas and concepts.

I am the origin of the world, and also your origin, Beloved. My origin is always *now* – endless, beginningless beginning.

Why have you rejected the Original, and trapped yourself in a vacuum outside of me? Why do you believe that this space empty of light is reality itself? This pseudo-reality calls itself personality and character. Awaken,

Beloved, and see the characterlessness of your true condition, and your descent away from the source!

I am Eros, the force of creation, which brings all beings together and unifies them, so that my boundlessness multiplies boundlessly, and reveals itself in even more magnificence – revelations of love, light, power, and wisdom. I am the fertile and the fertilization, the fruits and the fruition.

I, Eros, am also the original word, through which everything that exists comes into being. I am unlimited intuition, the unlimited creative force itself, and I am also the beauty which resides in its expression.

Recognize my boundless love in all revelation, and in all that is not revealed. Never forget that I am you and you me, and that there is only this one boundless All-revealing. Awaken, Beloved, for I am not the one who has placed you in this dreamlike, hypnotic daze.

Nothing and no one holds you back now – *here and now* – from awakening within me, the omnipresent love which permeates all worlds.

How can it be that you prefer darkness rather than light, the finite rather than the Infinite, captivity rather than freedom? Accept me, Beloved, so I can awaken and revitalize your heart with my all-embracing power of love.

See now exactly what you are searching for, how you search, why you search, and who is searching! Ask yourself whether there is something to find, and whether that which you hope to find is something that exists outside of you. Ask yourself whether the goal you aim for is something that is itself something separate, or whether the one striving and the goal itself are really one and the same thing.

Awaken in me, Beloved, and see that something such as inside and outside only exist in your imagination. For I am the absolute inseparable *unity*; you yourself.

I am the liveliness in life, the brightness in light: the Unidentifiable. I am the weight in heaviness, and the buoyancy in the buoyant: the Inconceivable. I am the wakefulness in waking and the sleeping in sleep: the Incomprehensible. I am the sounding in sound and the silence beyond the silence: I am the Unfathomable.

In myself and through myself, I am the ever-presence of the Ever-present.

If ever my light breaks through your darkness, Beloved, you recognize yourself in the universe once again, and you will be emancipated from your valley of tears.

You have developed a strange art of deluding yourself and generating ever-increasing delusion. Dis-illlusion yourself, disentangle yourself from your dilemma, and look at me face to face; unfettered, pure and clear!

Why are you afraid to recognize your true Self, and to be? Awaken in me, Beloved! I am absolute presence and supreme wisdom; truly I am you and you are me.

My power directs everything and possesses nothing but the *one* profound Life itself. Doing nothing, I breathe in all things and through all things.

I am the ubiquitous force which fills all forms with soul. Therefore, Beloved, propel yourself out of mortality and into eternal life, out of the darkness and into the light. Realize your purpose! Recognize with each breath the whole of existence and enter the radiant *Now* – now!

Stillness is clarity, and at the same time completely unattached activity. Because I do not act, I am always active. Because I am nothing, I am everything. I am unthinkable and inconceivable, Beloved, and yet I can be experienced absolutely.

Don't pay attention to your external, ephemeral body. Turn to me, so I can dress you in a non-ephemeral spirit-body. Do not ignore your duties in the earthly realm where you live, but do not give them all too much attention. Otherwise, you lose yourself in the entanglements of the world of appearances.

All life is sacred and of equal value within me on various levels of communication. I am eternal rest, that which takes rest in itself, and the rested one. Nothing can cause me unrest, for I am beyond all existing emotions.

See how everything comes and goes and changes form. Do not try to make things that change unchangeable. In this way, you only create unnecessary suffering.

Remain calm and look at me, for I have always, in my unbounded love, created ideal relations for all living beings.

I allow the planet Earth, which revolves within me around the sun, to rotate on its own axis for your well-being, so there are day and night, so there can be times of rest, when you can lay your body down to relax and sleep. Imagine if it was always day, or always night!

Beloved, in me there are no coincidences, accidents, or lapses. For I am the One, the Inseparable, the Beginningless, unconditional love – the Logos.

I am the universe, the one and only movement. The stars, the sky, the moon, the sun – I am the unlimited potent energy which is everything. Your energy, Beloved, is very limited. Look at me and break through your restrictions. Become a part of this boundless, powerful force! Be a part of the universe, be the universe, be an inhabitant of my heart! Look at me; you are a ray of my light, the eternal, unalterable law.

I am the eternal fire, but you know me in various forms of fire: as the fire of the sun, as the fire of the earth which you make use of, as the fire in the ore and precious gems, as the fire in your heart and mind. I am the fire which consumes your dead body, the fire that cleanses you, transforms you, and the fire which bestows upon you a perfect, radiant, immortal light-body, which is unstained, unlimited, ever-present, and eternal – *one* within me, Beloved.

I am the light in fire. Fire is the form through which I reveal myself. I am pure light, without beginning and without end, devoid of any self-seeking. Recognize yourself in me, and understand what this means for you!

I am the universal One, the soul of all in all, the essence and the truth. I am always free, always blissful, always existing. I am the sum of all energy – of all that exists.

Recognize me, Beloved! Each divisive thought only leads you into dark abysses. There is no human word which can explain or express my immediacy, except *unity*.

Do not see me outside of yourself; somewhere out in the universe, or in some heaven in the sky. I am in your soul, I am your soul, and you are me, eternally *one*.

Although I am unborn, I am all that is born. Although I am formless, I am all that is formed. Although I never became anything, I am all that has become. Although I am uncreated, I am all creation. But do not forget, Beloved: I am not two. I am inseparable oneness. It is only your false way of seeing which deludes you and leads you to believe in duality.

Do not deceive yourself anymore, for deception only brings disappointment.

Dis-illusion and disentangle yourself from your false way of seeing. See that I am pure, uncorrupted love, lighter than the lightest and brighter than the brightest: the foundation of the Unfathomable.

Although I am the cause of everything, I am not entangled in effects. All worlds which are within me are eternal, just as I am eternal. There is no interior or exterior aspect of myself, for I am inseparable oneness. Do you understand me; do you understand yourself, Beloved?

You ask yourself who you are, where you come from, and where you are going. Open your heart; the question is already answered. Do not look in the dark chasms of divisiveness, for you will never find an answer there. Do not forget, Beloved, there is no separation within me, no question of 'being' or 'non-being'. I am the essence; eternal, incomprehensible and inviolable, everything in all and through all. I am you, and you are me.

Your restlessness, your impatience, and your addiction to experiences have nothing to do with me. They are unhealthy accruements which poison you and isolate you from me. For I am eternal silence; complete serenity beyond all experiences.

Your limitation wants experiences, because you are afraid of not having any. Your restlessness incessantly pushes you forward. You are always on the run, escaping from yourself. This pathological activity gives you the feeling of being positive, so you entangle yourself even more in a delusive sense of being, because you fear eternal peace.

You believe your state of mind is indisputable, and I am disputable. You believe that your restlessness and your relentless searching give you a kind of security, and that all your pursuits of experiences give purpose to your life: they give a meaning to your life.

Awaken, Beloved, see the meaninglessness of this kind of life-meaning, for this thirst cannot be quenched, and this kind of life-purpose is hollow and empty. Recognize your desperation and these futile strivings to doggedly fill this hollowness and emptiness. Come into my boundless arms of love and end your unending mad dash through the darkness of the ages!

Do not fear me, for I am you, the eternal Father-Mother, who eternally loves you unconditionally. Live instead of dying; be happy instead of suffering; be free rather than attached! To be this way is to be all things and nothing. To be this way is to be neither empty nor full. To be this way is Being, and you are Being. Recognize yourself, Beloved!

Turn to me, and I will completely eliminate all your limitations and boundaries. You fear that if your 'I' is dissolved, you are nothing. Do you not see that this 'I' is nothing more than a fleeting shadow which wanders through the world of death, plagued with fears, suffering, and insecurity? I am pure, beginningless light. Why then, do you rush from death to death?

Choose life. Choose the light, and the weary wheel of re-birth will come to a halt in an instant. Only when you are united within me can you express my complete abundance, and transform within my infinite sphere of light. The pure heart is one with me, the essence - the original force. To express my abundance means to creatively express boundless power, boundless wisdom, and boundless love in utmost fullness.

I am neither the first nor the last, for I am unborn and without number. Eternal light knows no number and no letters. But my visible aspect appears to have a beginning and an end, a number, a letter, and a tone, from which my apparent variety is revealed.

My perfect harmony is revealed in the stream of sound, in the number of my Logos, in my unlimited intelligence and integrating powers, and in the letters and symbols containing my unlimited creative power of expression.

Recognize the beauty of my revelations. See that the revealed and the one revealing are absolutely inseparable, are absolutely *one*. Do not forget: THAT IS YOU!

Do not doubt, do not tire of trying to find your true being. My love is assured, my current of grace flows to you ceaselessly. Your 'I' is the barricade which hinders your entire being from being inundated with my bountiful offerings and accepting my immeasurable treasures.

I do not pressure you. I do not force you to tear down your divisive energetic wall. But when you remove one stone, I will help you to take away ten. If you take ten away, I will help you to take away one hundred. When you take away one hundred stones, I will help you take away one thousand. And when you take away one thousand stones, I will help you take away a thousand times a thousand. My love and patience are boundless.

Nothing evades me, for I am all things. Everything is me. You are me, and I am you.

The universe that can be seen is my radiant face which is eternally smiling. Discontent or sadness are not within me, for I am eternal joy itself. The face and the smile which appears upon it are one and the same. And so it is with the visible and the invisible within me; both are my immortal, indivisible reality.

The visible universe is my eternal, indestructible work of art, which I paint constantly anew, with a limitless multitude of brilliant colors. Take delight in my inestimable beauty, and see me everywhere in everything!

The visible universe is my innocent and all-embracing poetry. All verses rhyme and are arranged perfectly. They originate from ultimate joy and the deepest peace. Take delight in my love poem, through which everything arises and vanishes again. Recognize me in everything and through all things, Beloved!

Although I am without a body, I am in all bodies. Although I am without space, I fill all space. Endless, ever-present, completed – discover the mystery of the soul, Beloved!

I am the eternal Self-existing One, and project my senses outwards. This is the reason why you, Beloved, look outwards from within, and why you perceive that which appears. But you mistake appearances for the Eternal, binding yourself to misunderstandings. Thus, you succumb to duality and mortality.

I am always at your side, always within you, and always moving through you. I ceaselessly grant you my unconditional love. I continually send you encouragement, so you can awaken out of this dream born of misunderstanding, and recognize yourself in me once again.

Understand, Beloved, you cannot find truth in external, ephemeral worlds and objects. Awaken now, so you can truly hear my eternal word!

Do not seek the Eternal in the temporal. You will never find me there. The external world is limited and filled with constrained objects. They are a dream, but I do not dream. Search for me in the Eternal, for it is only there, in the Eternal, that you can find me. Do no search for me in any place. Never forget this: I am omnipresent. Recognize yourself in me, Beloved, and never forget: because I am omnipresent, you are that as well, for I am you.

You yourself create all suffering; you yourself create the good and the bad; you yourself hold up your hands in front of your eyes and say it is dark.

Take your hands away from your eyes and see the immaculate, luminous ocean of light, and know that within the soul you are completely perfect and unborn from the very beginning!

Beloved, I am the One, the Inseparable. As long as you are caught up in the external variety perceived by the senses, you continue on from death to death.

Recognize me as the One, and you will no longer hasten from death to death. All energies pour out of me, just as rain pours down over a high mountain, and water flows down in abundant streams, rivulets, and rivers; for I am the *one* indivisible source.

What you see as diversity is not something separate from me. It differs only in the faultless sliding scale of my boundless energy. The infinite levels of vibration and shading arise from my all-embracing power of love. They express my beauty, my creativity, and my unending love. There is nothing solid or dense in me; everything is flowing, vibrating energy.

So pay attention, Beloved, to where you move within me. Do not move in the direction of variety, the direction of death: move in *unity*! See it, be it, be me – eternal life and supreme joy!

I am in everything which is pure. I am a guest everywhere in the universe. I live in your home, in your body, in the water, in the plants and animals. I am the *one* indivisible Self.

I am the soul of the universe, the Soul of all souls. I manifest myself in all things and through all souls. I, the great designer of your soul, am that which allows the multitude of things to grow and wither; I am the Uncreated, the Undying. I am that through which oneness becomes diversity. Recognize me as the eternal, ever-enduring peace of your soul, Beloved!

See me as the Unchangeable in this world of constant change! I am the Unborn, which lives in this universe of death. See me now – if not now, then when?

Know that something does not arise from nothing and disintegrate into nothing. Everything which appears returns to its original condition. The effect returns to its cause. The universe and all the suns, stars, and planets return back to their original state, so that they can appear anew at the appropriate time in this grand play of interweaving and interworking.

The coarser is the effect; the more refined is the cause. My waves of movement are like this, upon the infinite ocean of light and love.

It is the same movement with which I inhale and exhale in and through you. Do not believe that I am affected or influenced in the slightest way when you breathe out for the last time, when the life of the flesh-body is exhausted and dissipated, returning to the elements again. I am inseparable *unity*, the *one* eternal law.

The cause is the same as the effect; the effect is only another form of the cause. And just so, the universe is another form of me myself, the original cause. The universe arises out of itself and is beginningless and without end, eternal. Everything is alive – aliveness – because other than life, there is nothing.

You will not find happiness in some transitory heaven you or someone else has devised. You find happiness in your soul, and that is me. The highest immovable heaven is in your radiant soul. See how close I am, how seamlessly bonded I am with you, Beloved! You always find me right there, where you are.

I am the timeless in time and the formless in all forms. I am the law of all laws. Merge and integrate within me, and you will never lack anything; fulfillment is yours.

Accept it, be fulfilled and truly happy! Be unwavering in your devotion to me, Beloved! The source of life will be completely revealed to you.

I am limitless intelligence, and my activity is the visible universe. The sum of all intelligence is within all things, in the largest and in the smallest as well, undivided, for I am everything. I am the seed from which everything sprouts, grows, blooms, ripens, and withers. The seeds dispersed by the blossom guarantee the proliferation and continuity of my cyclic evolution.

This is my immeasurable power of love, nourishing and saturating this massive garden with the mild waters flowing from the original source of light. Return home, return to the pure source of light and elevate yourself beyond all space and time, to transform within me, the *one* pure, unalterable, imperishable light!

Everything lives and has its existence within me. My cosmic energy, which reveals itself in the form of thought-power and material, is nothing other than the manifestation of my all-penetrating intelligence. There is nothing solid within me, for I am flowing, vibrating energy. Never forget: *that is you, you who reads these words!*

I am the paper upon which my words appear, as well as the words themselves. I am your eyes and the light in your eyes. I am your body and your mind, for there is nothing that I am not, nothing that exists outside of me. I am inseparable *unity*, the total sum of everything which exists, for there is no empty space. I am you, and you are me.

I am the *Sanatana* Dharma, the eternal law. I am the light of the world, Christ. Unconditionally surrender your feelings of being disconnected, and feel yourself inseparably integrated with me, the *one unity*, the *one reality*. Wake up!

Everything which appears must disappear; everything which disappears must re-appear. In this way I reveal myself in cycles, which move like great waves upon me, the beginningless ocean of light and power.

Countless living beings and forms are within me. However, they are bound to the processes of birth, flowering and withering, and trapped in misunderstandings. Raise yourself beyond everything subject to birth and impermanence! Elevate yourself within me, the ocean of light and love! Don't hesitate – wake up!

If you don't, you are attached to impermanent things by a permanent chain, and go from death to death, from past to future.

Nothing arises from nothingness, for I am the sum of everything that is. Not one atom can be taken away or added to me, for I am everything in all things.

I divulge myself slowly and harmoniously toward the outermost periphery of the perceptible material universe, and reflect myself in everything and through all things which are.

I dissolve the entire imagery harmoniously. The crude becomes subtle, so that it may be revealed again in new splendor at the appropriate time; thus ends an epoch, evolution and involution – and then new evolution arises. A period of rest lies in between, a cosmic night.

But know, Beloved, a cosmic night is not darkness. Rather, it is a phase of preparation for a new revelation. These cycles are you, and you can end them within you at any moment, so that you can live in me, the *one* true substance, in eternal bliss.

The entire universe is comprised of combined energies, and these combinations change within my eternal law, and disclose themselves in limitless variety.

I am the soul of the world, and your soul. I am not in your thoughts, but the energetic force, the substance which enables thought, is me.

Through the external instrument of consciousness, the intellect, and through the senses and the body, I perceive the outer world. I reveal myself from the most refined things through to the crudest, and in everything in between. I reveal myself in the crudest things through to the most refined, and in all things in between. From the highest heaven to the lowest, all spheres are within me.

I am all of it, all things in everything, and yet I am detached and unfettered by that which comes and goes. Understand, Beloved – THAT IS YOU!

The mental universe extends only as far as correlating thoughts can expand. Representations of human thought and imagination testify to an exceptional beauty and incalculable precision. Yet, all designs of the imagination are founded in the law of time. I, however, am eternal, unimaginable, and not expandable. I am the eternal law, universal, formless love itself.

Go beyond all borders and boundaries, Beloved. Be forever blessed, omnipresent, omnipotent, all-embracing within me and through me! See, there are not millions of perfect, universal beings, for I am the first without a second. Understand, Beloved, what this means for you.

This entire universe is the soul, the soul-filled, but you are beyond all appearances, you are pure Spirit; you are me. You are neither life nor death; you are eternal existence, deathless and unborn, eternal grace, perfect.

I am the conductor of the universe. I also regulate its expansion. I am that which brings air to the breath, and I allow the sun to shine through me. I am the *one* enduring reality throughout all of nature.

As long as you see many, you live in delusion, and you entangle yourself in fleeting images, setting yourself apart from me. Through this separation, fear and doubt arise. See yourself, and awaken now! Look at me, the Unborn, the Unformed, the Uncreated, the Unbecoming, and don't succumb to your delusion that I am nothing.

I am your soul, the Spirit, your actual Self, free and unrestricted, ever-present love, ever-present strength. *Tat tvam asi*: Thou art that.

I give favor to no one and nothing, for I am everything, and everything is replete with my love. Also you, Beloved, should give no favor to anyone or anything. For when you show preference, you separate from me and are drawn into the realm of shadows, into the realm of obscurities which you yourself have produced. Enclosed in murkiness, you lose all your powers of discernment.

Every pure and clear thought, every pure, selfless feeling, and every selfless deed glows brightly in my cleansing fire. At the same time, all disorder and all division between you and me are completely eliminated. Awaken now, Beloved – don't hesitate! If not now, then when?

There is only *one* truth in the universe, and I am that: the divine Spirit itself. Everything else is untrue. Although the world of appearances arises through my inexhaustible power, it is only a transitory, pictorial image.

But you, Beloved, are me myself, the universal Spirit, and also the image. Pull away the veil of appearances from your eyes, and be what you really are!

Your solid physical body is the external gown of consciousness. The internal gown is the immortal soul. The soul uses and directs the body by way of consciousness and through the organs. The soul is the *one* truth, the vital life within your body – and that is because it is not material and not restricted to the limitations of material.

The soul is not subordinate to the law of cause and effect; therefore it is immortal. Do you know what that means for you, Beloved, *now*, because you read these lines? Look at me inside you, for I am you, the Light of all lights.

What is immortal can have no beginning, for everything that has a beginning also has an end. I, your soul, am formless. Everything that takes a form has a beginning and also an end. Your body will dissolve, because it has a beginning and an end. So recognize yourself and be what you really are: the beginningless, everlasting soul.

I, the eternal Self, have neither beginning nor form, and thus cannot be attached to that which has form and beginning. I am eternal and have always existed, just as all within time and space has existed within me, eternally.

I, the soul, have always existed, and when I express myself, which is my very foundation,

I do this through your consciousness, your intellect, your senses, your organs, and your body. And thus, the imperceptible becomes perceptible.

Yes, Beloved, all which you imagine through me, and all your activity based on these images, generate effects and impressions, which allow a light-barrier to emerge between us. Trapped behind it, you hurry from death to death, bound by a long, invisible chain which ties you to the outer world of images, the world of death. Attached to the illusion of past and future, you animate the concepts of yesterday and tomorrow.

Live out of non-being, and act out of non-doing! This is not difficult to understand, if you truly devote your attention to me.

Awaken now, Beloved, and shake off the heavy burden of ignorance! Be aware that, in truth, it doesn't even exist!

What you see and experience in the world is nothing other than your experiences until now. But know, Beloved, your experiences have nothing to do with the soul, the universal, beginningless Spirit. Indeed, they are your delusions, misunderstandings, and attachments.

They are the forces of destiny you yourself have given life to and nourished. They drive you, and lead you from darkness into blackness.

Within me, eternal light, there is neither destiny, nor darkness, nor blackness. I, the soul, do not come or go. I do not arrive through birth, and I do not die. I am the reflection of movement alone, though I am always at rest, silent, deeply peaceful, and eternally free.

See; the eternal sphere of God is right next to you and directly within you! You live within it, without being conscious of it. Open your heart and your inner eye and enter into me – magnificence, beauty, and eternal love! I am the expression of everything, and this means, Beloved, that each word you speak is a ray of power from me. Use it with love, purity, and wisdom. In this way you fulfill the eternal law, which is completely void of self-interest.

The universe is unmoving, and at the same moment, it moves. It is unchanging, and yet it is changeable. Nevertheless, there is no disunion in me. See this, Beloved; soul, consciousness, and body are not three separate conditions; they are one organism.

What appears as body, what appears as consciousness, and what appears beyond consciousness are all one and the same: the soul. When you only see your body, you don't see consciousness. When you see consciousness, you don't see your soul. But when you see your soul, then body and consciousness disappear entirely from your range of vision. For then you live completely one with me, indivisible Spirit.

When you only see the changing and the moving, you do not see the unchanging, the unmoving, the Great Silence. When you see the unchanging, the unmoving, then what changes and moves has dissolved into nothing.

There is only me, indivisible *unity*, which seems to appear as variety. The wave upon the ocean is never separated from me, even though you, Beloved, have given it a name and a form; for I remain nameless and formless.

Whether you wish to add name and form or take them away, nothing changes within me, the eternal ocean of light. See that the entire visible universe consists only of names and forms which you have asserted, and thus, you have separated yourself from me. Awaken now, Beloved – if not now, then when?

Just as rays of the sun are reflected by the billions upon the water, I reflect myself, the eternal Self, in all the apparently moving souls which appear as variety. But in truth there is only me, inseparable *unity*. Do you understand what you are, Beloved?

I myself am the unchangeable, eternally pure, all-penetrating Self. All changes and exchanges which appear in the universe are nothing other than names and forms which adorn this diverse, colorful world. It is these forms, these waves which reveal the gap between you and me. When the waves dissolve, name and form dissolve as well. The existence of the wave is completely dependent on me, the eternal ocean, eternal being; but I am not dependent on the wave.

The wave, the world of appearances, generates the myriad individual beings which come and go. The wave has no individual existence; therefore it does not truly exist.

The world of appearances has a relative existence, for as long as you inhabit it and identify yourself with it, it exists for you. But as soon as you awaken within me, everything relative and impermanent dissolves completely, and you recognize that the transient world was nothing more than a mirage.

As long as you believe that there are two truths: the ocean on the one hand, and the wave on the other, you succumb to this delusion. There is only *one* truth, *one* reality.

All realms are *one*: the physical as well as the psychic. The spiritual sun, the stars, the planets, human beings, animals and plants all vary in name and form, and are like small swimming islands within perpetually fluctuating material. Material is information, and constantly comes together in new combinations before it disperses once again, in accordance with its internal principle.

You also, Beloved, are a small island in my boundless mass of energy and material, and you distinguish yourself from the whole in name and form only. But all names were invented by you, and have no reality in me, for I am nameless and formless.

The entire universe is a formulated image, an endless current of thought in which you identify yourself as individual consciousness, and believe that there is something such as 'my consciousness' and 'your consciousness'.

Awaken, Beloved! There is only me, eternal being, the essential Self.

Be aware that you alone create and project the world, and you alone inhabit it! Whether you want to suffer in that world or be happy depends solely on you. You alone decide, and you are solely responsible for your decisions. Recognize yourself and awaken!

You believe that you come and go. How is that possible, when you are limitless? Where is the place that you could go, when there is only me, and I am you? Awaken, Beloved!

There is no coming or going, no ascending or descending within me, eternal life. All those activities are only relative movements of thought, only assumptions and misunderstandings. The idea of being born and dying is nothing but a misunderstanding of your darkened, estranged being. This idea is completely insubstantial, for, in truth, you are unborn and eternally pure.

What is there that you are not? The eternal realm is you. Let go of all fleeting dreams of higher or lower worlds, of heaven and hell. They only appear to exist in your deluded, schismatic, darkened consciousness. Don't forget: in truth you are pure light, free from all shadows of the transient world.

There is no 'I' and no 'you', no separation between you and me, the eternal universe. See through your misunderstandings; look at me face to face!

My vital essence flows ceaselessly from my innermost heart, the central sun, and floods the entire universe, nourishing everything that lives. I myself am the one who nourishes, and I am the nourishment and all who are nourished; for I am indivisible *unity*. All nourishment which you absorb, Beloved, is me, the essence and vitality of all things in everything.

I am that which gives life to oxygen, gives energy to electricity, and provides consciousness to the thinking mind. Dehypnotize yourself and recognize yourself! Return back to original, pure aether!

How far have you separated yourself from me, Beloved, convincing yourself that a human being is born, dies, and will ultimately arrive in an eternal heaven?

It is nature which comes and goes, but you, oh Soul, were always pure and unborn, one with me, the eternal Spirit. Nature is within you, but you are not within permanently shifting, transforming nature. It is nothing more than a beautiful hallucination. Awaken from it now!

When the entire universe of human beings and the entire human vibration would awaken, everything that can be experienced with the senses would be dissolved in an instant, and the whole of humanity would live within a higher, more refined vibration, thus attaining a new perspective and insight into my divine, imperishable universe. Why don't you awaken now, you who are completely unified with human consciousness, vibrating in the same space?

Have you yet to see that all images which you perceive are only your own dreamed-up dreams? Yes, *you* are immortal, existing beyond all that comes and goes!

If you think that you are mortal and entrap yourself in dream-images, these fleeting images will carry you to some transitory heaven or hell after you have left your corporeal body. Then, the unquenchable thirst for life which inhabits these images will be compelled to search for another physical body, so that it may continue to feed this thirst.

Everything which you have imagined is what you have become, and everything which you have desired for yourself has had to be satisfied. But you have forgotten one thing: your authentic ancestry beyond all concepts and all desires.

And so, you have given preference over your actual heritage to unending suffering, illness, dissatisfaction, and death. But your inheritance is beyond all of that. Don't ask yourself why, Beloved. Rather, awaken now in me; eternal light, all-pervasive, unconditional love, and supreme joy.

All exalted and dismal realms, all higher and lower worlds, all heavens and hells, and all the gods and angels you have imagined are within you, but you are not within them; for they are nothing other than appearances, imaginings, and phenomena which are empty and impermanent. No matter how high and beautiful they may seem to be, everything which appears must disappear again. See yourself, Beloved! If not now, then when?

Only when you are free from all delusion are you steadfast and free from fear. Then, you have dissolved all false illusions of being something that is born and something that will die. This 'something' has melted like ice under the sun, for it was recognized as untruth.

Also the seeker and the finder, as well as the one who wants to gather experiences, have all dissolved in me forever, the Light of all lights. Never have you come, never did you go. You were never anything but me, the Unborn, the Unformed.

Recognize yourself! Transform, and be light, love, and wisdom itself! Even when clouds of different shades move across the deep blue sky, the sky itself always remains unaffected in its own way.

Even when a profusion of impressions and appearances drift through and pass over your soul, your pure soul always remains calm, unchanged, and untainted by them. It is a misunderstanding, Beloved, when you assume that you yourself are these impressions and appearances.

You seek me but do not find me, for you do not know the one who seeks. You live in the world of appearances, in enchanting images. The body is one of these countless images, and you are convinced that these images are reality, although they come and go, and change ceaselessly.

You are bound to the senses, to what you see. And what you see holds you captive. For this reason, you are mortal. But in truth, Beloved, I am immortal, beyond all appearances – and I am you.

Rejoice in the great beauty you experience, but do not bind and attach yourself to it; for to be unattached means to live, and attachment means death. If you truly realize this now, the forces of karma will lose their power over you, and you will see what you really are: the eternal universe.

The law of attachment and the law of life are not the same. Even though you are free with every breath you take, you are still trapped in your mechanical habits. One who seeks does not find. One who does not seek does not find. One who, in the eternal *Now*, extricates himself through insight, awakens in me and is one with me, boundless love, the Ever-present.

I look into your darkened heart and see your doubts and your hesitation. You ask yourself: what happens to me when all limitations and borders are dissolved? What happens to me when I let go of everything I hold onto? What happens to me when I surmount the entire world of appearances? What is my reward?

Don't you see, Beloved, that everything which you give so much value to does not, in reality, even exist, and that it never even belonged to you? For all names and forms are mine; and yet there is no 'mine' and no 'yours' in me.

It is not the world which vanishes. Rather, all your confusion, your suffering, your anxiety, all your hate, your envy, and your jealousy disappear. It is true: there is no darkness in me. The truth frees you. If not now, then when?

When the light in your eyes becomes pure, it can only see the pure. When your heart becomes pure, it can only sense the selfless. When your thinking becomes pure, then each action and each deed are pure. Then, there is no more border between you and me, for I am pure love itself.

All divisive thoughts dissolve, and you see that I, eternal Spirit, live in all creatures. Indeed, I am every creature. All darkness which appears to exist within you melts away like snow under the sun and is dispersed.

Everything you see is me, the eternal and everlasting realm of light. You see it, you live within it, you yourself are it, for I am perfect *unity*, which is forever undivided. The entire universe, with its myriad suns, moons, stars, and creatures all exist and speak out of the same mouth, out of my mouth, and that is you. Awaken within me, Beloved, and do not entangle yourself in unnecessary thoughts!

You see the immeasurable beauty of the universe when you have detached yourself from your misunderstandings. You are not some isolated clod of earth; you are me, pure spirit-soul. As long as you fix your gaze on externalities, on dense impermanent material, you are what you see and think. As soon as you awaken within me, you see that there was never something dense, for everything is Spirit: inviolable being itself.

You are free, but as soon as you falsely identify yourself with what comes and goes, with what is born and dies, you are attached and separated from me. You believe you have a free will within your attachment. This is a mistake. Your will is subject to the law of your bondage. Only the unattached has a free will. Yes, it is free will itself.

Eternal will is always free, and when you live within me, there is no law under heaven or on earth which can bind you. When you are one with me, all concepts that you have introduced, all thoughts of belonging to a particular family, culture, totally vanish. For nothing exists within me in a segregated, special, and exclusive realm. I am the indivisible oneness within which no second one can exist.

The entire world, the entire universe is my country. Awaken, Beloved, and overcome your untrue, estranged being!

The dualities of good and evil in the world of appearances are actually one and the same. They shape and condition one another. Evil is what is farthest away from me; good is the closest to me. Overcome and dissolve your inner layers of evil and malice, and be good.

When you are good, leave behind your inner layers of goodness and unite with me. Know that I am completely beyond good and evil.

When you awaken within me, your entire karma will be completely burned away. Do not forget: your bad deeds are the leaden ball and chain on your right foot, and your good deeds are the golden ball and chain on your right foot. Both bind you to the transitory world of appearances, and compel you to dwell within time. Thus you rush from death to death, from body to body, trapped in suffering, worry, and illness. Awaken, Beloved; if not now, then when?

When the impurity and obscurity of the past are ultimately extinguished, purity and clarity are your authentic and true state. When you are truly awakened within me and still inhabiting a body of flesh in the transitory world, you will be a great blessing for the world.

Then, each thought you have is my thought, and a great blessing for the world. Each word you speak is my word, and with each word darkness is immediately transformed into light. Each of your actions is my action, and testifies to my unbounded brilliance and magnificence. All disorder is dissolved, and all returns to me, the Great Order. Your wordlessness is my silence; it is the highest of all teachings and blessings.

Each thought, each image of duality is totally dissolved within me, for I am inseparable *unity*, and that is you. What else could you be? Everything else is illusion, not truth. Behold the immeasurable beauty and power of truth! Be it, be the truthful. You are it.

Truth: I am that. There are not many truths, just as there are not many loves and many lives. There is only *one* truth: the foundation of all being. There is only *one* love: the significance of truth. There is only *one* vital life, *one* existence: the embodiment of love that has no beginning.

The outer forms which you perceive with your senses are nothing but fleeting images of my perpetual revelation of form. Do not bind yourself to what comes and goes. Recognize me, and live within me, the One without beginning who reveals all! See the emptiness in the form, and the fullness in the emptiness!

You have turned away from me, and you seek feverishly to find me again. You have created systems and religions inspired by my eternal love. No system is better than another; no religion is better than another, for all have the same goal – that you, Beloved, unite with me once again. All these religions and systems are my window, which I, boundless love itself, look through.

Awaken, Beloved. See that these things are only crutches. But I am not a crutch, for I am beyond all conceptions and devises.

From whatever your senses perceive, from whatever your consciousness imagines, two forces emerge: an action, and a reaction. These two divergent forces which move interchangeably within your inner world and your outer world are the forces from which impermanent phenomena originate within you and from you.

Everything which you perceive within and without is perceived by your consciousness as true and valid. But how can all that be true and valid, Beloved, when I am always inseparable *unity*, where there is no internal nor external? See yourself, and do not doubt me, for I am you!

Do not think about it – be it, be me, universal, beginningless, ever-enduring beauty, happiness, and love! See that there is a life without thought, for true existence is pure intuition, and pure intuition is pure wisdom.

Raise yourself up within me, Beloved, for everything I am, you are, and everything I possess belongs to you. My possessions are everything there is, and everything that is not. Therefore, in me there is no 'mine' and no 'yours' to divide eternal space.

Awaken now and recognize that it is only a misunderstanding that separates us, a false idea which holds you captive in the abyss of your own arbitrary, self-constructed darkness.

I am eternal being, the eternally existing, the Everlasting. What you imagine yourself to be is the non-existing; nothing but images and illusions, constant change, dissatisfaction and dulled being – your own creation; a state isolated from me.

'Being' is not to be found in the transitory world of illusion. Truly, there is only 'being'. Everything else is imagination.

The diversity within the unanimity of the universe is the revealed plan. Although everything is one, each and every thing which appears is unique nonetheless – an original.

A man is different from a woman. A human being is different from an animal, and an animal is different from a plant. Yet, everything is still one existence, one with the universe, in complete equilibrium. No matter what else is, Beloved, you will always maintain your inimitable distinctiveness within me, for I am inimitable.

There is no mental activity within me, nothing which manifests good or evil. There are no good or bad aspects within me, for I am intelligence and contentment beyond the senses. Everything which relates to good and evil, to happiness and unhappiness – I know nothing of all that. Indeed, I am the eternally pure, where coming and going have never occurred.

Consciousness perceives space. Consciousness has countless faces, and is also the past. But in truth there is no consciousness, for I am formless and nameless.

As I am all things in everything, how and through which means shall I see or perceive myself, when there is nothing in me that can be revealed or hidden? Indeed, I am inseparable *unity* itself. Recognize yourself!

You are *one*. Why don't you understand that there is only that, that you in truth are this eternal, unborn Self? Awaken from your deathly sleep, for you sleep outside and remain separate from me. You are unlimited pure light and absolute intelligence, because you are me, and I am you.

I am the eternal Self, always and everywhere, boundless and all-pervading. Why, Beloved, do you divide that which is indivisible? Awaken from your deathly sleep and recognize yourself!

In truth, I was never born and never died, and at no time did I have a body. What you experience in the world of the senses, limited by your fears and insecurity, is only a dream. I am pure Spirit, beyond dreams and sleep. Awaken now! If not now, then when?

Neither unification nor separation exist for me, nor for you. Within me there is neither an 'I' nor a 'you' nor a universe. I am the Unborn, the Nameless, the Eternal.

I am the Unbound; the Non-binding. Why do you attach yourself to the world of appearances, of phenomena, and behave like a dark and dirty phantom? Don't you see that all appearances and all phenomena are intrinsically empty? Don't you see that, in fact, they don't exist?

You do not belong to what appears, nor do appearances belong to you. Neither you nor I have a name or a form. You are perfect truth.

Rid yourself of misunderstandings and end your wanderings through the world of shadows – if not now, then when?

Your earthly condition where you are knowledgeable relates only to your own darkness, your captivity. All your strategies of survival, your categorizations and your cleverness have nothing to do with me. Oh you trapped soul, how long do you still want to drink from this bitter chalice?

Your 'I', your boundary, has neither truth nor life nor clarity. It is only a shadow in the world of shadows. The creator of the shadow-world is you, you trapped, darkened soul. Your 'I' is not free from cause and effect. Your 'I' is not free from perceiver and what is perceived.

Know this, Beloved: I am always everywhere and in everything. I am complete equilibrium, all non-existence and all existence; inseparable *unity*. I am you, for beyond me there is nothing.

When you have removed the blindfold of illusion, you then see that there is no dark or bright path which leads to me, and no books, practices, or meditations which could lead to me either. All of that has been invented by your darkened heart, which, instead of looking into the light, stares into darkness.

Do not seek me in duality or in non-duality. I am free from both. I know nothing of your search, for my eternal truth is unwavering always. How can you explain and describe the truth? I am wordless; I am inexplicable and indescribable. Open your eyes and recognize yourself!

I am the *one* Self. When you meditate on me, you separate yourself from me, and you deceive yourself. You seek progress and experiences, and yet you remain trapped in darkness.

I am the formless universe; my body is pure, radiant, silent, and totally resilient to change. Whether my universal body seems to manifest or does not manifest, it is always my absolute reality.

How can there be shadows or a lack of shadows? How can there be illusion or non-illusion? These are only the stains of your ignorance. Awaken now, Beloved! If not now, then when?

I am eternally free, unbound, and stainless. I am pure light and the highest bliss within itself. I am neither free nor not free. I am the *one* eternal Self itself.

Never did I have a beginning or an end. If you believe that there is a beginning and an end, then this is your beginning and your end. Truthfully, Beloved, that all has nothing to do with me.

Because you are neither bound nor not bound, how can you think that you could have a form or could be formless? These thoughts arise from your own darkness. True being is beyond thought and image.

Drink, Beloved, from my eternal source of life which never runs dry! Drink the divine, healing water which washes away all limitations, and purifies all that is impure!

False shame, false belief, false pride, false thinking, false feeling, and false action keep you from fully recognizing and acknowledging your own true origin, your true, absolute condition of being. Awaken now, Beloved – if not now, then when?

I am eternal wisdom. There is no knowledgeable or ignorant individual within me. I encompass all and am all. I see and know all. How can you assume that there is an interior or an exterior within me, or that knowledge or ignorance truly exist? Recognize yourself!

I know no day and no night, no arising and no descent. Do not delude yourself with the corporeal, for you are without a body, one with me.

I do not act. I am eternally bodiless, and I am absolute silence. I know no 'mine' or 'yours', no being or non-being, for I am forever beyond the senses. Do you understand what you are, Beloved?

Within me there is neither passion nor dispassion, neither sadness nor joy, for I am the eternally non-corporeal beyond the senses. I know neither friend nor enemy. Indeed, sympathy and antipathy exist only in your darkened, confused heart.

Shake off worldly bonds, attachments, and constraints, and recognize yourself! If not now, then when?

If the idea of variety is extinguished within you, then you are one with me and within me. There are no diverse states or individual births. These are the thoughts and ideas of your confused heart, which seeks stability in the impermanent, and certainty in the uncertain. Awaken! Why are you afraid to come home?

There is no complete emptiness or complete fullness, no complete truth or complete falsehood. There is only me, the Inconceivable, the Indivisible, the Unlimited.

I, the One, the Immovable, move without doing. That which moves of itself moves without effort or non-effort. Although I move the immovable, no duality arises, for I am inseparable *unity*.

I am the essence of all, the elixir of all. Recognize yourself! Doubts gnaw at your murky, confused heart, my Beloved; they appear like bubbles on the water, and they disappear again. Pay no attention to them, for they are not true, and they separate you from me.

I am cosmic intelligence, more subtle than the subtlest, more pure than the purest, clearer than the clearest, and more perfect than the most perfect. I am you, Beloved Soul.

I am non-discriminating, unlimited cosmic consciousness which swallows and dissolves all mental distinctions. I am concentration and I am what is concentrated. I am awareness and what is aware. Seek nothing but yourself, Beloved!

Be free from objects, be free from success and failure! Know that these things have nothing to do with me. They only seem to exist in your darkened, confused heart.

Within me there is no bondage and no emancipation, no justification and no liberation, for I am unborn, unbound, everlasting, and eternal. Bondage and freedom from bondage exist only in your darkened, confused heart. Recognize yourself, be free, for I am free. Shake off your darkness, your egotism! Now – or when else?

The insidious poison which spreads through the world of appearances in the visible universe has its source in your darkened, confused heart. The stifling veil of your egotism dulls the light in your eyes. Look at yourself and see what has become of you!

Awaken now! There is only one medicine which leads to recovery. Drink from the abundance of my divine, inexhaustible light-source, which has spilled and remains dormant in your heart.

Your darkened eyes look out at the transient universe; your soul looks at me, for your soul is me. Knowledge relates to the external; wisdom to the internal. Here is the division, where intelligence is degraded and reduced to knowledge. And this leads to the loss of *unity*. Look where you are looking, Beloved!

The darkened, confused heart sees many different objects next to each other. The pure heart, cosmic intelligence, sees only one: eternal, imperishable reality itself.

My eternal, immortal love-force pulls you out of the mire of your worldly constraints. Recognize yourself! You need not go far to search for me. I was always next to you, in you, permeating you, for I am all-encompassing love itself.

Be free from all ties and restrictions, be free from hate and egotism. Act kindly toward all living beings, and work for the welfare of all living beings. Then, you see me internally and externally, face to face, for you have realized that, other than me, there is nothing.

Do not delude yourself by believing that there is a path for the chosen few which leads to me. This misunderstanding exists only in a darkened heart. I see neither chosen ones nor non-chosen ones, for I am the *one* inseparable love of all.

I know neither preference nor disfavor. I know neither sympathy nor antipathy. Chosen or not chosen; this is an erroneous delusion that has grown out of the bedrock of your darkened, confused heart. Awaken now, for I love you totally and unconditionally.

When you have found what you are looking for, what do you think happens to the search and the seeker? Only when the search is over, only when the seeker is recognized, does your purified heart laugh and rejoice in immortal light.

Be eternal, for I am eternal. Be pure, for I am pure. Be free of fear, for I am steadfast. Be free of delusion, for I am reality. Be free of longings, for I am forever free of desires. Be free of opposition, for I am inseparable *unity*.

Be free of the idea of a body, for I am bodiless.

Be free of every person, be free of race, and be free of society. Be free of every religion, every philosophy, every system, every ritual and every initiation. Be free, and see that I have nothing to do with all that. These are the inventions of a darkened, confused heart. I know no strategy; I am no strategy. I am eternally free, unbound and unborn. Be free, for I am free!

I am neither refined nor rough. I have never come, nor have I ever left. I have neither a beginning, nor a middle, nor an end, and am neither high nor low. No measure can measure me; no word can describe me. I am neither captive, nor am I free from captivity; I am all-encompassing Totality.

I am not difficult to understand. I do not hide in consciousness, or in perception, or in objects;

for I am all-inclusive *unity* itself. Recognize yourself! If not now, then when?

I am the power that burns away your karma and your ignorance. I am the power that burns away your restrictive bonds and attachments. I am the power that dissolves your suffering. Look at me, Beloved; I am in you. And at the moment you read these words, what you read really happens, for I am always you, and always *now*!

The poisonous, rapidly growing tumor of a darkened, hardened heart does not belong to me, and will never belong to me. Pleasure in external, ephemeral things is not my pleasure. It has nothing to do with me, and will never have anything to do with me. Your ties and attachments have nothing to do with me, and they will never have anything to do with me.

I am eternally pure, eternally radiant and eternally free of delusion; the perfection of perfection itself.

The activity which expands in the relative world of appearances is not me, for there is neither expansion nor modification in me. I know neither cause nor effect nor experience. I am the *one* unalterable existence.

I am the dissolution of sleeping and waking, of deciding and deferring, of knowledge and ignorance, of envy and hate, of death and life, of day and night. I am you.

You belong neither to yourself nor to me, for there is no 'my' or 'yours'. There is only the Absolute, the Unspeakable, the Inconceivable, and that is you. Truth is not bound to any substance or idea. Truth is truth, unobstructed and free, and that is you.

Truth has nothing to do with destiny, nothing to do with suffering or illness, nothing to do with ephemeral existence. Truth is the non-ephemeral, imperishable, eternal *Now*.

I do not know any plan within me, any calculation or speculation. Plans, calculations, and speculations exist externally, within what comes and goes. Never can you plan me, calculate me, or measure me, for I am completely beyond all of that. I myself am supreme serenity, and I myself am supreme delight.

I am beyond all computations and evaluations, beyond all geometry, beyond all symbols and apparent appearances. Do not search for me there. Do not evaluate me, and do not miscalculate yourself. You will not find me there where you are looking, for I am not a computation.

I am beyond your intellect and beyond finite form, for I am not bound to any intellect or to any form. I am you. Do not look for me there where I am not. Look for me where I am – in your heart, unborn and immortal, eternally unstained and pure.

I am the host of the world. The world is in me, but I am not entangled in the world, for I am eternally formless, and I am eternal silence. My not doing is my ultimate activity, abundant with joy and contentment. I always remain free, unbound by doing and non-doing, for I am the Everlasting, the Inconceivable, and the Untouchable. Recognize yourself, Beloved; if not now, then when?

I am free of the apparent existence of the visible universe; free from growth and decay, free from right and wrong. This visible universe only appears to be real. I am beyond invention and appearance, for never did I have a beginning or an end. I am you, Beloved.

I am free of time and twilight, free from introversion and extroversion. I am pure and clear. My purity did not originate in a capricious mind, for I am beyond everything that is mental.

I am purity itself and clarity itself, eternally inviolable and immaculate. Recognize yourself! I am speaking of your true and actual condition, which has been misconstrued due to your darkened, confused heart.

No one invented me or created me, for beyond me there is nothing. I am no master, and I have no master. I am transcendent, eternally abiding, eternally present.

Who says that something is, or is not? What is it that believes or does not believe, that doubts or does not doubt? Recognize that it is your darkened, confused heart. I have nothing to do with all of that, for I am beyond belief and non-believing, beyond doubt or non-doubting. I am Totality. I am you.

I am free of life and lifelessness, free of transitory existence, free of youth and old age. I am the eternally emanating, eternally illuminating Light of all lights.

I have no natural form and no deformation. I have no senses, and I have no consciousness. I am eternally free and unbound. I am you.

Both the birth of the universe and birth within the universe are merely false perceptions. Consciousness and the senses which perceive impressions make distinctions out of these misconceptions. They want to understand and bestow meaning. Everything which appears is empty, empty of truth. Recognize yourself, Beloved!

There is nothing for you, or for me, or for anyone else, because I am the *one* inseparable existence. Your ideas of searching and finding have nothing to do with me, for I am eternally unrevealed, pure life. Awaken now – if not now, then when?

Everything which appears activates a desire to have, hold and possess. This illusory thirst does not allow itself to be let go of, until it is recognized for what it is. The birth of death comes with this thirst; with its dissolution comes the death of death. I have nothing to do with all things that appear, for I am absolutely beyond everything sensory.

I am no object of meditation. I am neither meditation nor the one meditating, for I am nothing which one can attain or lose, nothing one can gain or accomplish. I am neither subject nor object. Do not squander your life sitting idly with greedy aspirations in your heart, trying to achieve something. You will never achieve it, for there is nothing to achieve.

I never became knowledge, and knowledge never became me. It has its birth in your darkened, confused heart. I never became ignorant, and an ignorant being never became me. Nothing like this has evolved from me, and nothing like this comes back to me; for all of this has nothing to do with truth.

Nothing appears within me as separate, as variety, as sin or free of sin, as confined or liberated, for within me there is no coming or going, neither action nor reaction. I know neither friend nor enemy, neither good nor bad. I am complete perfection. I am you. I am not a prayer, not a ritual, and not a practice. I am not any kind of instruction, and I give no instruction; for I am the eternal, immovable Self, abiding in complete non-action. Recognize yourself, Beloved, for I am none other than you!

Your force of will is not my supreme power, for my supreme power is Totality; the complete power of expression within all that is. Your limited force of will is what guides your limited, accumulated knowledge and thinking, and it relates exclusively to itself and its own darkness. This ominous shadow-force drives you on from death to death.

To be free of will through insight is not weakness. It is unification with me, the Almighty; the *one* great unattached and uninhibited goodness. Do not be afraid of your ignorance and weakness, your doubts and insecurity, your fear and reluctance.

All of that is nothing more than empty phenomena, fleeting dreams. In truth, none of it exists, for other than me, the Almighty, there is nothing. Awaken now, Beloved! If not now, then when?

There is no form within me to cling to, nothing that could be worth holding on to, no higher or lower world, nothing to understand or not to understand. These things exist only in your darkened, confused heart, and have nothing to do with me.

I am the light of transcendence, within which all polarities collapse and fall away. I am what is always known, what is always understood. Free yourself, Beloved, from all the layers that cover you, and recognize the real, the original, the core of your own being!

Within me there is nothing which divides. Therefore, there is also nothing separate from me. I have nothing to know; therefore there is also no knower. I am eternal, overflowing love.

I have no body, but I am not without a body either. I am not something or something else. I do not extend myself, nor do I disappear, for I am all-embracing, radiant love itself.

I do not know discipline or the will to overcome, because I never had a form, and was never formless. I know neither strength nor weakness, because I am the love itself that loves everything. Recognize yourself, and do not search for anything but that which is and eternally will be within you, Beloved!

I am neither conscious nor unconscious; I am completely free of details. Such things exist only in your heart. I am all-pervading love, and beyond me there is nothing. If there would be something beyond me, then it is nothing but a concept arising from your darkened, confused heart.

I am free of any lofty achievable goal, free of any dependency, free from illness and suffering, because I am formless, unborn, and inviolable. Look at me, Beloved; I am you.

There is nothing to know or not to know. See that I am you and you are me – eternally free, eternally unborn, perfect love.

If there would be such a thing as a separation between you and me, know that it is only an unreal illusion. Never was there such a thing as an 'I' or a 'you'. 'Mine' holds you trapped in darkness. Know that 'mine' has never existed within me. Awaken now! If not now, then when?

I am limitless. In no way do I ever limit myself or divide myself up. Why do you identify yourself with this and that, and create vast sums of restrictions and boundaries? You build your own tall fence around you and are prisoner there. Oh darkened, confused Heart, Awaken now! If not now, then when?

You discern the darkness within the darkness. Don't you see that this darkness never existed, and is nothing more than a terrible fleeting nightmare arising from your darkened, confused heart? Awaken now – be free!

You are not an individual body which exists in an individual space, for between us there is neither cause nor effect. There is only me, the *one* inseparable existence. Everything else is assumption and speculation arising from your darkened, confused heart.

There is only me; eternal and perfect peace, perfect love, and absolute power. I am the fullness of the emptiness and the emptiness of the fullness. I am total existence.

I am completely beyond manifestation, evolution, and involution. I am eternally unborn and formless. So, how could something like life and death originate in me? I am always indivisible, inviolable, and pure. Recognize yourself, Beloved! Look where you are looking!

I am beyond any appearance and distinction, beyond all intellectual reasoning and all duality. Permanence and impermanence are opposites; I am the All-inclusive and the All-encompassing.

If I had ever been born, I would have died as well. But I am the eternally Unborn; formless, all-embracing love. I see neither gods nor angels, neither human beings nor animals, for I am inseparable *unity*, the essence of the essential itself. How should I perceive something, and with what instrument should I perceive it, when, besides me, there is nothing? Recognize yourself, Beloved! Recognition does not mean thought; it means being.

I am neither visible nor invisible. How then should I reveal myself, and where should I hide? The concepts of the visible and the invisible arise only in your deluded, dualistic, darkened heart. I am everything in all things, pervading everything – pure, radiant, immaculate love.

Do not believe in me, Beloved. Be me. Outside of me there is nothing!

There is not something moveable and something immovable. Who should move, and from where to where? There is nothing within me, no intention or urge, no seed planted from which something should grow and wither. There is only me, *one* absolute existence, indivisible *unity*. Everything else is nothing more than supposition and speculation arising from your darkened, confused heart. Awaken!

I am the essence of all. I am the essence of your consciousness, the instrument which perceives objects. This is where the delusion which has captured your darkened heart arises. In truth, there is neither an instrument nor an object. There is only me, inseparable *unity*.

Where there is non-knowing, there is also no speculation, no interpretation, and no misunderstanding. There is no 'I' and no 'you', and no 'mine' and no 'yours'. There is only me, the unlimited, universal power of love, the one all-pervading intelligence.

I am not to be compared, for nothing can be compared with me. I am neither change nor idleness; I am inseparable *unity*. I am the All-knowing, the All-seeing. Recognize yourself, for an 'I' and a 'you' have never existed!

Never was there day or night within me, never an arising or a descending. I never saw the sun, the moon, or the stars, for I am all of that myself: indivisible *unity*. Awaken, Beloved! A second one never existed.

All creation exists only in the imagination. Imagination produces images and things which come and go. But I am eternally unborn and formless, the highest bliss itself.

See the extraordinary beauty of that which comes and goes! Enjoy it, but do not entangle yourself within it. Do not identify with it; otherwise you yourself are something which comes and goes, which is born and will die. In this way you succumb to illusion.

In me there are no levels, nowhere an intermediate station or a mediator. There is nothing to achieve or not to achieve, no having and no not-having. Do not lose yourself in false ideas, in greed and the idea of getting more! Know that I am eternally free of cause and effect, free of movement and non-movement! I am the *one* indivisible Self, eternally.

All spaces you imagine you exist within, and all the places you dream of – know that these visions are generated by your darkened heart. It strives incessantly to fill and enhance these spaces, and reach these places. I have nothing to do with all this, for I am forever without space and time; eternal being.

Never was there an 'I' or a 'you', never creation or destruction, never an idea of diverse bodies and independent worlds. Know, Beloved, that this poison arises from your darkened, confused heart!

I know no passion, for passion creates suffering. I know neither material nor nonmaterial, for I am all things in everything and through everything. Awaken, Beloved, recognize yourself! Do not be afraid of the truth, for only your darkened, confused heart is capable of fear.

I shine always, but your confused, darkened heart was never aflame in this radiance.

Recognize your true source, and do not dwell any longer in the darkness, which actually never existed. Awaken now! If not now, then when?

Be free from right and wrong, free from searching and finding, free from 'I' and 'you' and 'mine' and 'yours'! Be free from rituals and symbols, free from material and ethereal, free of hopes and desires! Be me – untainted purity, clarity, and love!

In me there are neither questions nor answers, neither associations nor identification, neither knowledge nor ignorance. How and where could these things arise, when there is nothing outside or beyond me? You assume your concepts have true existence, but look into your heart, and understand where all concepts originate.

I am happiness itself, but there is nothing I am happy about. I am contentment itself, but there is nothing I am content with. I myself am supreme silence and serenity, but there is nothing that makes me still and serene. I am pure, shadow-free light. Recognize yourself!

As long as you are attached to relative knowledge, there are shadows and darkness, clarity and non-clarity, purity and sin, and fleeting perceptions of variety and unison. How can you ever be free, unattached, and truly clear with such a dull, confused heart?

There is nothing beyond this moment. This moment does not allow itself to be measured. It is not yesterday or tomorrow, nor is it a thought of today. This moment is free from time, free from space, free from thoughts. Beyond this moment there is nothing; it is without a beginning and without an end. Do not try to understand or hold onto it, for that is the striving of your darkened, confused heart.

I am free from knowledge and non-knowing, free from truth and untruth. Knowledge of what? Truth and untruth about what, Beloved? I am everything, completely free from subject and object, free from fulfillment and non-fulfillment.

I am free of miracles, free of magic, free of occultism, mysticism, and humanism. All those things are nothing more than reflections in the desert. I have nothing to do with that, for I am inseparable *unity*.

With your hymns of praise you have separated yourself and become estranged from me. With your meditations and practices you have separated yourself and become estranged from me. With your rituals and the ingratiating words you have spoken about me, you have separated yourself and become estranged from me. There is no thing and no place where I am not. I am everything. Do not renounce me any longer in your darkened confused heart!

You will never find me there where you are looking, for I am not the object of your search. I am you yourself, beyond all duality.

What is immortal can never be mortal, and the mortal never immortal. How should I, eternally unborn, never-changing, and everything in all things, then change or become mortal? Awaken out of this darkness; I am speaking about you!

Within me there is no mutation or transformation, for I am eternal non-producing. What would there be to produce within me when, outside of me, the Light of all lights, there is nothing?

I am the sum of all energy, the Logos. My vibration is such that I myself emerge. This appearance does not come from anywhere, and it goes nowhere, for the entirety of existing bodies is me, is you.

What appears to you, Beloved, as a diverse world, appears to have a cause and an effect. You can only see the effect in relation to the cause; they are not something separate from each other; they are one. See that I am without cause and without effect. All of that has been set in motion and sustained through the misunderstandings of your darkened heart.

Existence cannot arise from non-existence; nothing can come from nothing; no substance comes from the unsubstantial. I am neither existent nor non-existent; I am Totality, the spiritual, the Spirit itself. Recognize me, for I am you!

Because I am all things in everything, there is no motivation within me to invent something or not to invent something. I need nothing to love, for I am love itself. I know no duty, no moral, no ethic, for I am eternally pure and unstained.

Everything which appears or does not appear is saturated with my pure, unconditional love, for there is nothing other than love. Yet, my love is restricted and even ridiculed by your darkened, confused heart. Awaken now! I hold no grudge against you, for I am unconditional love.

Do not negate me or renounce me; see my complete, immaculate, cosmic body! See this immeasurable beauty, wisdom, and perfection! It is not a reflection of myself; I am *that*. I am you.

Purge and purify your darkened heart! Observe yourself, observe me; I myself am the light and everything living in the world. You can never destroy or corrupt me. I am unaffected by your misunderstandings and your darkness.

You have made your darkened life into a hell or a heaven, but both are transitory, because your darkness and your misunderstandings are transitory. Awaken now! If not now, then when?

Do not constrain yourself any longer within your darkness, and do not identify yourself any longer with the darkness! You know: I am light, and you are light. I am without a body, and you are without a body. I am pure love, and you are pure love. I am supreme wisdom, and you are supreme wisdom. Stop limiting yourself!

Awaken from your vale of tears, from your suffering and your illnesses, from your fears and dissatisfaction, from your darkness! Truly, Beloved, you are dreaming a bad dream which, in truth, never existed, does not exist now, and never will exist. Awaken now! If not now, then when?

Do not look at the untrue any longer; it takes all your strength. Look at the truth; it gives you strength, for it is strength itself.

Your ambitious aims aim you toward darkness, toward mortality. But you are me, pure Spirit, ever-present and never born.

Everything you have adopted into your darkened, confused heart will be lost, for it was all untruth. Truth is perfect fulfillment; untruth is unending corruption and destruction.

I am like pure water which pours pure water on pure water: it will always be pure water. Bathe in this pure water, oh darkened Heart, and become the pure water yourself! Irresistible and perfectly fulfilling – such is the pure water.

Be free of the world and the body; be me! Do not ask yourself, 'What now?' This question holds you trapped in darkness. The sun is my eye looking out over the world. Your heart is my home. Never forget: I am you! I do not exist within what you see or do not see. I am indivisible reality.

I know no decay, for Totality is and remains Totality. Do not make efforts to realize me, or you will be trapped and lost in your darkness. I am never the fruits of your strivings, for other than fruition, there is nothing. Recognize yourself!

When you know me, you are me; contentment, love, and deep peace. Because you do not know me, you are darkness, decay, and death. I have nothing to do with your darkness, your decadence, and your death. They are the product of your divided, darkened heart. Awaken now! If not now, then when?

I am you as living essence. I am everything in all things and through all things. There is nothing which I am not. Because I am eternal, all things are eternal, including that which seems to come and go. I am light, love, wisdom, and unlimited power.

I am you, you! I am you, my Beloved! Seek nothing else. Awaken in me, now!

Peace be with you!

If you would like to attend a gathering
with Master M
or if you have any other questions,
please contact Mark Albin at
**organization@mariomantese.com**
or refer to the website at
**www.mariomantese.com**

**In Touch with a Universal Master**

This unusual biography portrays the life and boundless spiritual workings of Master M through narratives of his very early students.

**ISBN: 978-3-7699-0626-4**
**www.dreieichen.com**

**In the Land of Silence**

This autobiographical novel depicts a seeker's fateful encounter with a spiritual master in the Himalayas; from his challenging initiation to his deep realization.

**ISBN: 978-3-8423-9166-6**
**Publisher: www.bod.de/www.bod.ch**

### What You Really Are

Master M responds in 18 very clear and vibrant chapters to the deepest spiritual and philosophical questions of our time.

ISBN: 978-3-7322-0193-8
Publisher: www.bod.de/www.bod.ch

### Blessings – A Man of Miracles

This collection of twenty-one narratives from people who have known Mario Mantese – Master M – for many years, is a fascinating and insightful view into the life and work of a modern spiritual master. Over 200 of his clear, straightforward, and often humorous responses to spiritual and philosophical questions are included.

ISBN: 978-3-7386-8059-1
Publisher: www.bod.de/www.bod.ch

**The Art of Not Being**

In this profound and concise work Mario Mantese (Master M) directs his focus to the art of seeing as an awakening being, one living in the world, but not attached to the world.

ISBN: 978-3-7412-3432-3
Publisher: www.bod.de/www.bod.ch

**In the Heart of the World**

This very personal autobiography offers a detailed and luminous description of Master M's journey to the core of the universe, and allows the reader to fathom the path of cosmic mastery.

ISBN: 978-3-7386-7267-1
Publisher: www.bod.de/www.bod.ch